VIA FOLIOS 115

Because I Did Not Die

Because I Did Not Die

Nicole Santalucia

Bordighera Press

Library of Congress Control Number: 2015948533

COVER ART: Deanna Dorangrichia
"Red Lantern Series VI: after Caravaggio–David With the Head of Goliath."
(18x14 inches, pastel and charcoal on paper)

Printed in the United States.

Published by
BORDIGHERA PRESS
John D. Calandra Italian American Institute
25 West 43rd Street, 17th Floor
New York, NY 10036

VIA FOLIOS 115
ISBN 978-1-59954-094-8

TABLE OF CONTENTS

Because I Did Not Die

The Cannoli Machine At The Brooklyn Detention Center

The cannoli machine in the Brooklyn Detention Center is for the visitors;
my dad waited in line when he went to visit my brother.
He didn't know he'd have to empty his pockets,
take off his pinky ring, and untie his shoes.
This is the first time I saw my father afraid,
but he wasn't too afraid to stand in line
with all the other fathers
in front of the cannoli machine.
He ate two or three and noticed
a little white cream filling on his cheek
when he saw himself on the surveillance camera;
he noticed that his white t-shirt was washed too many times
and was starting to turn grey,
that his socks didn't match.
I didn't know this was how fathers were made.

Brother

Somewhere in the world someone is dying
and somewhere else someone is sleeping.
I know where both of these people are;
they live in Manhattan.

There are times when I think both are me,
but then I wake up and realize I didn't drink
the night before. It was just another wet drunk dream
wishing for the past to repeat itself,
to give someone else a chance.
When I throw these wishes into an empty well,
I hear them echo as if I threw a thousand dimes
and all of them bounce off each other
mimicking the sounds of birds
and these birds remind me
of the pigeons that might be landing on your toes
as you lay stiff on a cardboard box
cut open and sprawled out on 88th Street
and Broadway. Brother, you are not
the only person who has left yourself
for dead.

There are thousands of pigeons
shitting all over this city.
This is why I left,
and somewhere else,
maybe on 83rd Street between
West End Ave. and Riverside Drive
in apartment 2E,
one of the pigeons that landed on your

dead toe is cooing on the window's ledge
annoying someone who can't sleep,
or maybe this dirty bird knows our mother's
address and it is trying to wake her up
in the middle of the night
to tell her that it's finally
over, that she can stop worrying
if we have ever overcome
our fear of the dark.

Oh Brother

I learned how to fly
so that you could see me hover over Manhattan
dropping cheeseburgers like bombs.
I aim for West 88th Street
between Broadway and West End Ave.
Grease splatters on your windows
and the meat bounces off rooftops.
The birds are at war,
let them win.
Now climb down from the tree;
those branches need to grow.
Come down from there
and stop acting.
Your audience is human.
The sky above this island
has emptied itself for you.

Golfing

I'd swing, grunt, then whip the nine iron into the sand pit.
I always missed the ball and threw my club.
It flew through the air like a helicopter,
made a divot in the ground as if a small piece of Mars
dropped from the sky.
My left hand soaked with sweat
in a baby blue leather golf glove.
I'd run into the woods,
look for golf balls that other people lost
and find my brother's ghost teeing off,
he'd aim for the eighteenth hole,
his nose scrunched when he swung.
It's like he was waving a thirty-pound silver sword,
just a little too heavy,
and instead of making him stronger
after each swing he got tired.
I never thought he'd be strong enough
to swing back at life.

My Mother Called

to ask me not to write poems
about my brother who is in prison.
I didn't get a good night's sleep.
My new neighbor, Georgia, snores
and wakes up early to do laundry.
She takes off her underwear
and washes it every day.
I fall asleep fully clothed and wear
my shoes in bed because I don't want to separate
from the possibility of leaving.
Georgia has a drawer in her bathroom
where she hides cans of beer,
hoping she'll forget where she put them.
I wonder if my brother waits in quietness,
or if he has to fight for his food,
or if he's reading the Bible.
I tell my mother not to worry,
that I'll write about how I started
having bad dreams because my neighbor
is loud in the middle of the night.

Truth

Even now I want to tell her to get a life,
but the sadness gets caught in my throat.
Kind of like the sadness that spilled
on the floor next to the bed,
or was that your grown son shitting himself,
or your wishes drowning
in the warm glass of milk I refused to drink
because I didn't want to go to sleep?
Instead, I listen to the ticking sound
of branches scraping against the window;
I choke every time you call me.

The Prisoner

There are some people who will outlive cockroaches;
you are not one of them.
There are others who will have an allergic reaction,
and others who will climb out their bedroom window
to sit on the roof of their house
and wait for the moon to disappear into a bloodshot sky.

You might press your hand against the cold cement floor
or fall from the top bunk and wonder why the smell
of the river is everywhere now.

It wouldn't make a difference if I sat outside your jail cell
and waited or if you tried to run from the prison yard
that's on the side of a mountain;
not only will the guards aim for your head,
but you'll have nowhere to go
because everything is under water.

You are afraid of the Mexican gang and I'm afraid
of the men who are gliding by in rowboats
trying to find out if any kids drowned in the river
that swallowed their houses.

In 1993 The Sex Was Cheap On Pine Street

The smell of fresh bread from Dalosha's Bakery hung over the train tracks
where boys used to shine shoes, sell lettuce and newspapers,
where mothers stuck their heads out of windows over the kitchen sink
and blew whistles, called the whole neighborhood home for dinner,
served it on paper plates.

Where my father's childhood home burned down,
the green house in the middle of the block
with boarded up windows and red spray paint.
I can't tell the difference between people and piles of garbage,
where my body was tossed to the side of the road like a wet cardboard box.

The first time I drank too much I went looking for the green house
my father grew up in, the one that had a fenced-in yard,
a mound of dirt blocking the basement windows.
The one that was converted into apartments, then abandoned.
Where I found out I'm related to everyone in this damn town,
that my uncle Tom works the graveyard shift
and rides on the back of a garbage truck
picking up all the dead bodies
in black plastic bags before sunrise.

Where I found out that the bakery has gone out of business
and the earth tastes like homemade dinner rolls,
I've lost and found and lost the thirteen-year-old self
that stopped and looked both ways before crossing the street,
barefoot and hungry for a plate of spaghetti.

In Other Words

The words I didn't say are locked in the metal box on the shelf
next to a pile of folded crew neck sweaters in my father's closet.

These words are the dollar signs my mother says she sees in my eyes
when we talk on the phone years after I've stolen

my brother's ski mask and hid in the beer aisle at the corner store
on Ackley Ave, my finger pointing like a gun under my sweatshirt.

The old lady working the register was scared of the sixteen-year-old girl
drowning in words she couldn't say: *sorry, thank you, help*.

The words *Big Bear, Old English*, and *Colt 45* lined the roof
of my parents' white Volvo station wagon. The police pressed me

against the window, pressed the words out of my bladder. The words
I didn't say the first time I got arrested were warm and yellow;

they are the pants I peed in. The words are in unharvested wheat fields
with other words. The words that made my fake gun real are in songs.

"Luck Be a Lady" is what I hear when I pretend to be the hitman
that my great grandfather was asked to be in 1922.

The getaway car didn't drive over the words that escaped the metal lockbox
when my father opened it, re-wrote his will, then closed it again.

I Remember When You Were Fat
And Smelled Like A Rotting Rotisserie Chicken

We passed each other on 76th Street. You were missing a shoe
and your sock was dark brown. It looked like a bag of mud
as if you were headed back to the graveyard
after taking a walk to get lunch
because that's what the living dead do.

I've already mourned you.
I was in the grocery store and saw the rotisserie chickens
slowly turning behind the deli counter.
I wasn't hungry, but a woman next to me ordered two.
I hope there are at least two pigeons
outside the bars of your jail cell.

Breaking News

The first time you kissed the tip of a sawed-off shotgun
god's tongue wrapped around your waist and pulled you
out of your skin—a puddle of beer on the floor instead of blood.

Outside, street lamps flicker and news reporters
can't get a clear shot; they're lined up at the front door
stepping over piles of hair—we pulled our hair out, clogged the drains
and I'm still in the bathtub wrapped in phone cords, my hands callused.

The newsprint on my forehead says something about how the town
of Johnson City has no money left in the budget for teachers,
that garbage pickup schedules have changed—and I worry
if anyone will tell our parents that they'll have to take the trash
to the curb on Tuesdays now.

My Mother's Teeth Are Smeared With Lipstick

There's no way to start this poem
without getting lipstick on it.
Everything in your pocketbook
is coated with a shiny red gloss,
even the dollar bills
have a pink sheen.
Your teeth are smeared
with lipstick, too.
I used to take the stuff
from your purse,
wipe it on my forehead,
and pretend that's where you
kissed me before I went to sleep.

When I Think Of War

I think of my mother
sitting all alone in a rocking chair
waiting for me to arrive.
She expects me to eat the dinner she prepared,
even though she hates to cook and is horrible
at cleaning the dishes.
There are always dried pieces of tomato sauce
on the forks in the top drawer.

When I think of war I see all the empty seats
at the kitchen table and realize
that no one gets out of here alive.

I don't imagine a battlefield when I stand over the sink
and rewash the dishes. Instead, I hear
How was the pasta?
followed by
Why won't your wife visit anymore?
She is secretly saying that she hates
the feeling of being replaced.
I shrug, go back to the sink,
and put away the silverware while it is still wet.

Witness Of Consumption

She is in a dark room sitting in an armchair
as if in her grave this will be her position.
The desperate experiment is the repetition:
the bourbon-color sky, the bourbon-color clouds,
the bourbon-color house with bourbon-color rugs and walls
and the sound of ice freezing in the freezer,
the crackling sound of bourbon
in a glass on the kitchen counter the color of bourbon.
The melted ice and turkey sandwich on rye
is what we remember finding
after the death of your mother.
And her demise was not sudden,
in fact it was the slowest death.
It was like Death was born
then poured herself a drink,
sat on the couch
and awaited our arrival.

Hanging On

My mother
looks like a lampshade
because she is standing
behind the living room curtains
spying on the neighbors.
There is murder in the trees
on the corner of Beethoven Street
and Seminary Avenue.
I don't notice
the desperation
as I rip away at the earth
with the strength I inherited
from my mother
who warned me
about how the gypsies
have been out abducting little girls.
She says that my kidnapper
is just waiting for me
to show up.

The Coffee Table

If I could wake up anywhere I choose
it would be under the glass coffee table
smudged with crushed Viagra and baby aspirin.
My neck wrapped in my brother's black t-shirt.
There would be a cat named Mr. Peepers licking cocaine
off of my chapped lips and my brother rummaging
through a pile of dirty clothes. The clouds on the coffee table
would be our last pile of heartbreak.

And the blue fibers from the carpet
are falling out of my ears fifteen years later
as I pass the ringing payphone on 91st Street
and West End Avenue and step in wet pavement
where kids carve their mothers' names.

I'm searching for you on the way to pick up my clothes
at the laundromat, in the wrong city,
on the wrong day of the week.
Maybe if it were a Sunday
we'd both show up on our mother's front steps.
There would be chicken and mashed potatoes
and our mother, wearing all black, gripping a rosary
in one hand and nothing in the other.

In A Coat Closet In Endicott, New York

I woke up in someone else's car,
a 1983 maroon Toyota.
The engine was still hot.
I must have just arrived;
the house keys were in my coat pocket.
I went inside and started cooking dinner;
there were empty bottles of olive oil
lined up on the window ledge
above the sink next to the onions;
yesterday's mail sat on the counter,
someone left the radio playing,
and the fan blowing.
This is how people live in Endicott, NY.
My father's mother's voice is in the coat closet.
She must have woken up in the maroon Toyota, too.

The Things I Want To Believe

I want to believe that drunk men go to the bowery
and bathe in puddles,
that they drown in their own vomit.
I want to believe that my father
spent his childhood tied to a swing set
or that my mother was forced
to eat dinner in a dark coat closet.
I want to believe these things
because I need an excuse
for the time I robbed my parents,
I need an excuse
for the time I broke into their house,
crawled across the living room floor
and got distracted by the white fuzz on the carpet.
I thought it was crack and ate it.
I disappeared that night
with my mother's jewelry and my father's wallet.
I need to believe that someone else
has experienced what it's like to starve.
I need to know that drug addicts and drunks
don't die alone on their parents' floor
in the middle of the night.

Learning To Appreciate Insanity

I'm afraid I've grown to appreciate insanity,
but what worries me more is all the garbage
that's been buried.
I'm worried it will smell
and remind me of my first boyfriend.
Mathew was named after his father
and he was as tall as the Christmas tree
in the living room.
This Christmas tree wasn't one of those miniatures
or lopsided Charlie Brown trees,
it was really tall.
It stuck out of the garbage can
when we threw it out.
This was the same Christmas
cousin Ryan bit off his father's ear;
we threw that in the garbage, too.

Emptying Out The House

The only thing we found under her bed
was a note taped to the bedframe
that said who should inherit the mattress,
and in the top drawer of the dresser
there was another note
that had your name on it.
The lamp she tried to send you
home with every time we visited
had a note on it, too.
There was a list of names
on the liquor bottles
under the kitchen sink.
We never heard her mention
Bobby, Lou Anne, Madeline.
And there were picture frames
with price tags on them in her closet;
the receipt was in her wallet.

The least we can do is return these frames,
to put something back where it came from.

Someday I Will Learn Italian

So that I can go back to
the basement where you hovered
over the stove and hung the pasta
on clotheslines.
I'll go back and translate our conversations.
I used to think I was a ghost in the room,
unable to speak. But, I wasn't a ghost,
I was nine, maybe ten,
and I was always hungry.
The only phrase I could decipher
was *feedagurl* or *feedaboy*.
My brother and I were nameless
when you spoke to us;
your back was always turned.
Sometimes when you went to get
more homemade wine, or outside to pick grapes,
I'd sneak a sip of your drink.
I'd steal my own memories.

This wasn't the only thing I stole.
Years later, after you walked
out into the garden and never returned,
when your house was sold
and all the left over pasta tossed in the trash
and wine bottles passed out
at your funeral like wedding favors,
I stole mouthful after mouthful
until my lips were purple.
I drank myself into the future.
I predicted my own death.

Now, in this new life,
I haven't learned Italian,
but I do throw my hands around when I talk.
My mother tells me how much
I remind her of you,
and sometimes I wonder
if it was your breath that I stole.

Jealousy

I could have lied
when my mother asked me for the gun,
but I didn't want to
accidentally shoot myself in the foot.

It was an old ivory grip pistol.
I have no idea if it had ever been fired
or even loaded for that matter.

I just know that I couldn't sleep
with it under my pillow anymore.

I wanted a tattoo of a cheeseburger;
then I wanted to eat a lot of cheeseburgers.

I wanted to learn how to piss in a soda can
without making a mess.

I must have grown up under a pigeon's wing
and lived in the clock in Grand Central Station.

I learned, early on, that the wind pushes the past
against my chest and that jealousy exists on both the back
and front porch at the same time.
Jealousy exists in France and in New York;
it exists in my pants and under my arms.
It exists in the Hudson River
where they should put prisoners
on a boat that circles Manhattan.

The Idea Of Bread

There's no bread in the breadbox,
it smells of yeast and paper.
My father stores his receipts
in the breadbox.
He buys too many nails, bolts,
and hinges as if he's going to build
a dream with a swinging door
or a box made of old wood
that only stores receipts
and the idea of bread.

The house is sinking into the ground.
We must stand next to it
and push up
so that my father
doesn't suffer anymore.

Santalucia

I always thought my last name came from a boat
that sailed across the world
but I was confused
that was the Santa Maria

Not that my name hasn't traveled on boats
or shined shoes
or sewed the soles of feet
back onto soldiers
who've been shot down

Santalucia is the train station
and the train
it is the mountain
and the grazing cow

It is the boy scout
wearing his sash
the baker
and the bartender

It is the grapes and the wine
the cork and bottle
tucked in someone's suitcase
traveling through Italy

It is what I whisper
when I sit at the river's edge

In Johnson City Not All Of The Houses Have Basements

My first kiss tasted like grapes and got me drunk
in the basement
where they made the wine
where my lips opened
and the cold glass bottle swallowed me
it was an incestuous act

When I was twelve
I dreamt about shiny glass bottles
lined up perfectly on a shelf
I dreamt about thousands of blue
glass kisses in the basement

In Johnson City
not all of the houses have basements
not all of them have a place
where the men in the family
crush the grapes
where the little girls
drink the poison

In The Gardens Of Binghamton

Even the houseplants get public assistance in this town.
Everyone is thirsty.
The sex is cheap.
The wine is homemade.
If you're a twelve-year-old girl
living in Binghamton, New York
you're probably tied to a swing set,
watching the grass grow,
waiting for it to rain,
but the clouds don't let loose.
They just get darker and darker;
eventually the dry black sky consumes you.

This is how loneliness breeds
in the gardens of Binghamton.

Last Night

When we got home from Meghan and Brian's wedding
I found a crumpled up ten dollar bill
on the sidewalk in front of our house.
We must have just missed a drug deal;
the money smelled of sweat
and must have been gripped tight in the buyer's hand.
It was familiar,
the smell of money in the dirt.
When I picked it up I got nervous and wanted to run
in circles in the backyard with the neighbor's dogs
to forget about how on the way home
we stopped at the gas station to buy a newspaper
and milk for midnight cappuccinos,
how the woman working the night shift
started crying because she just lost her house
and how we felt stupid when we said sorry.
Last night we had our first dance
at someone else's wedding and my hands
and feet were sweaty.
I was afraid to fill the car with gas
even though I feel sexy when I pump it.
I was afraid because it was late
and I used to get lost at night in this town.
I used to sell drugs and drop wads
of ten dollar bills on the ground.

Another Ending

We stood on the train platform at 72nd Street and Broadway,
late for work, unable to recognize ourselves.
Me, wearing a suit and tie; you, a pair of strong boots
and long grey coat. A handsome man next to us
asked if we were sisters. Then, the woman at the café
asked for the third time in a week
if we were sisters. This is when I wanted
to grab you by the neck and kiss you hard.

Nine years later we no longer get on and off trains;
we are always late and stopping to get coffee.
I still want to consume you. I also want
to go back and find that man on 72nd Street.
I want to go find that woman who served us coffee.
I want to stand and wait for the train on Broadway.

This is just a story, one that I've returned to
as we stand in another town where no trains run,
where no man or woman stands near enough to question us.
We outgrew the tallest buildings and left the end
up to someone else; perhaps in a coffee shop two women
are meeting for the first time, or parting after their first date
and their first kiss was on the train
while we are repeating as many Octobers as possible
in another town where it rains most of the time.

Just In Case We Ever Get A Divorce

She was a beautiful bride,
although her face didn't look the same
as it did in the advertisement.
When she arrived in the mail,
after I washed the ink off her forehead,
I knew she'd be perfect for the job.

I ordered her with no intentions
of getting a new pair of boots,
but the mail order bride company
threw in a freebee.

I love boots;
there are about twenty pairs
in the back of my closet
covering a pile of mysteries.
I toss them there in the middle of the night
just in case we ever get a divorce.

Bitches On The Roof

I love the bitch, said the guy with no teeth.
Then, he took a swig from his can of beer,
climbed back up the ladder onto the roof,
and started hammering.

You can't live with that bitch anymore,
said the other guy with a bigger tool belt and two teeth.
The bitch won't even cook, said no-teeth man.

I sat quietly on my porch listening to these men bitch
as they fixed the neighbor's house. I secretly wished
their bitch-asses would fall off the roof,
and I wanted to tell them to stop bitching,
to take off their bitch costumes and strap on real cocks.

It was late May and the men kept coming to work on the house.
Sometimes they would wake me up. They slurped their beer and bitched
about their baby mommas. I started dreaming about tool belts
and memorizing their conversations as they hammered each shingle.

Now, it is June and I'm wearing my own tool belt and sitting on the porch.
Every once in a while I look next door
as if to agree with the men who re-roofed the house last month
and I want to climb on the roof and scream,
I love the bitch.

I Love What You've Done To The Bitch

Not just any old bitch, but the mother of all bitches. I want to run home and build a bitch out of popsicle sticks. I want to suck on frozen juice until my face is numb and then throw it all up. I mean, skinny bitches aren't just skinny, they have to work bitch hard to stay rail thin. I want to make a family of popsicle stick bitches. They will have cotton balls for heads and some of these bitch-stick-people will have bitch babies, just like in real life.

The Day We Got Married

It was like getting a fishing license or registering a boat
as if we were headed down to the Susquehanna
under the State Street bridge to look for dinner
on the riverbank or in the murky waters surrounding Binghamton.
The day we got married we went through metal detectors,
put our house keys in a bucket, handed them
to the security guard at City Hall.
It was like we handed over fistfuls of concrete on Hawley Street.
On our wedding day a fat cloud sat in an office,
didn't get up when the City Clerk opened the door.
The couple in front of us, George and Paul, exchanged
handkerchiefs instead of rings—they waited forty years
to give each other a faded piece of cloth,
a stand-in for freedom that's been shoved
in a back pocket.

Genealogy

My wife warns me about sitting on public toilets
as if there's fresh sperm waiting to jump inside me.
I never tell her that on long days my legs get tired,
that sometimes I carry a pile of books into the stall
and don't set them on the floor, that my skin makes contact.
And she tells me to go wash my ass. And I say,
I'm afraid to have children, too. This conversation repeats
about once or twice a month.

Every time I'm in a public bathroom
I think of names we'd pick for our children;
saints' names like Ita, Clelia, Madeline, Maria, Lucy,
Rosalia. I list all our crazy Italian aunts and grandmothers,
who had numb fingertips and eye sockets that ached.
I think about the Patron Saint of Palermo, Rosalia,
who lived in a cave and how our cave is no longer dark.

I think about how Saint Lucy's eyes were gouged out
before she was executed. Saint Maria Goretti said she'd rather die
than submit to Alexander and she was stabbed in the gut.
I think of how cousin Maria brings her drunk boyfriend
from Texas to Christmas dinner and how we all shut up
when he entered the room. And how my grandfather told me
that he was in love with another woman
before he decided to marry Nana.

Every time I enter a public bathroom I wonder
what it would have been like to gouge my eyes out and serve them
like Italian grapes to the children our grandparents would have had
if they married someone else.

Sidewalks

Her face reminds me of the sidewalks
in Times Square on New Year's Day
tired and stained after a lifetime of celebrating
with blackberry brandy
there's anger in the crevices
wads of chewed gum
and a policeman
a bad policeman
the kind who steals your wallet
helps you look for it
escorts you to the station
to file paperwork
then goes to the deli
and orders a turkey sandwich on rye

She only eats the crust of sandwiches
then feeds the rest to the birds
but the birds are not hungry
when they peck at the pavement
they chip away at the sidewalk
until their beaks are dulled
until someone walks by
on their way to lunch
someone who has been doing community service
cleaning the street on their hands and knees
scraping it clean with a razorblade

Ode To Maria

Husston and Wiebe share the title
of this year's golf tournament in Binghamton, NY
this is just as important as the headline
about gay marriage in this town
When I read the paper this morning
I thought it was funny how Husston and Wiebe
rhymes with fuckin' dweeb
then I realized that this was the golf tournament
sponsored by Dick's Sporting Goods
and how it was just yesterday
that my wife delivered a basket of cookies
for one of their raffle prizes
and that some fuckin' dweeb would win it
The thought of some guy eating my wife's cookies
makes me a little jealous

I realized the front page of the paper was folded in half
and I almost missed the article
about how the Sewage Board Oks Safety Inspection
Not only is this town going to shit
and fuckin' dweebs are winning golf tournaments
but my morning is dragging on
I'm drinking too much coffee
which reminds me of just the other day
when we were standing in line at the City Clerk's Office
and how I had to pee really bad
The bathrooms were locked
and I thought about you Maria
how you were the one who told us
in your perfect scratchy voice

to go get married
you are the one
who I always run into in the bathrooms on campus
because we both pee all the time
you know
all that limoncello and those double shots of espresso
Maria
you are the one who I want to run up to and say
I hope you are proud
I married a good Italian girl

Prostitutes

Maria, there's an ex-prostitute sitting at the table
in your poetry workshop at the university.
In fact, you had lunch with her the other day.
The two of you shared a turkey sandwich;
she put mustard on toasted bread for you,
and when you told her about your *agita*,
it made her feel safe; it was like caressing her on the arm.

Maria, your poem about not knowing
how to talk to the prostitute in New York City,
the poem about how you awkwardly waved goodbye,
blew her a kiss as you walked out of the bookstore
onto the street—that prostitute needs your poem,
so a little part of her will get off the street.

The Crack House

There are clouds in my handbag;
there are clouds when I look through the metal blinds
with the tip of my gun.
There are clouds in the living room
sitting on the couch.
There are clouds in the bathtub
where I fall asleep.
There are clouds in the night sky
and when I open the back door clouds leave;
my dog looks like a cloud
and I feel like a cloud about to let loose.
I look out the back door and more clouds wait,
they want to come inside because they forgot something
and the clouds begin searching
turning over furniture
pulling out drawers
opening cabinets
ripping apart closets
searching the medicine cabinet
and finding nothing except dust.

My Silver Spoon

The ball of tinfoil in my pocket holds fresh cooked crack.
It's like I am the pink and yellow paint
on the walls in the living room,
or the empty space in an ocean.

I go into the bathroom to shower, take off my pants,
place the ball of tinfoil on the counter,
lock the door and breathe; in my lungs,
it feels like steam from a boiling tea kettle.

In two hours, the sun will start to rise;
the tinfoil ball will have nothing left
and I'll eat it to make this moment permanent.

This is electricity. The mechanical seagulls need more power.
I need more power to throw myself into the open waters and not come back.
With every last bit of energy, I hurl my body at the ocean and miss.
The reflection on the charred silver tablespoon holds my face.

Because I Did Not Die

Because I did not die
from burning my fingers
on a glass crack pipe
the scars on my fingertips throb
when I wash the dishes
or shovel the sidewalk
for my neighbor.
There are days
that have gone missing
and tattoos dripping
off the body I left
on the corner of Carol Street.
A mile and a half
away from where I stand now,
at the university,
shaking hands with the Dean,
my lungs tighten
as if I've never
taken off the straitjacket,
and someone else's voice
escapes my throat, says, *thank you.*
And, I want to tell him
how I've never gotten the spiders
to stop crawling out
of my eyes and nose,
that they take over my face
in my sleep. How my skin
feels like cracked cement
in a parking lot
full of uprooted trees.

I want to tell the Dean,
who is congratulating me,
how I've been counting time;
how, when I lived in New York City,
Heroin Helen lived on the corner
of 87th Street and West End Avenue.
She was sprawled out on the sidewalk,
newspapers stuffed in her shirt and pants
to stay warm. Every morning,
for years, I stepped over Helen
because I couldn't save her.
I want to tell the Dean that part of my commute
this morning was devoted to her.

St. James' Basement

I bite the styrofoam cup, carve into it with my thumbnail,
and stare at a statue of Mary Magdalene just outside the restroom.
Why is she in the basement?
I think about how she's too close to the door
and if someone were to break in through the window
they would knock her over, her head would fall off.
In the large room people sit in folding chairs
arranged in a circle and they talk about miracles.
I spill a little coffee from my chewed cup.
On the way to the toilet I rub the coffee
on my forehead to bless myself.
Outside in the parking lot men rev their motorcycles;
they sound like a starving god and the tremors blur my vision.
For a moment I wonder what I did with all the money
I made as a prostitute. I wonder if Mary Magdalene
will mind if I use her hair to dry my hands.
I want to clean up after the drunks who showed up tonight
hoping for resurrection.

Ode To Alcoholism

The tree limbs in Recreation Park scratched my eye,
tore holes in my t-shirt. There are school buses
lining up in front of Seaton Catholic High School
on Monday morning while I rise from the shrubs,
rest my hand on Mr. Johnson's cold brass knee.

Last night, in Binghamton, NY,
I went to the Belmar Pub on Main St.
looking for someone to love and I choked
on Fitz's 90-year-old lizard tongue
and brown glass bottles with long necks;
in the bathroom my hair stuck to the floor.

This bar used to be a barbershop
where my grandfather worked, wisps of hair
were swept out into the street, into the dead
January night. The hair that had once fallen
to the floor now whips through the air,
it gets stuck in my lungs, and winter stays
inside me; the winter that whispers,
get the fuck out of here before it's too late.

Making Amends

I am not sure why I choose to sit
at the foot of the grave next to yours,
maybe because the name has worn off
the stone or because I'm still sorry
for breaking into that man's house and stealing
everything except the war uniforms
that were perfectly aligned in his closet.
I didn't take the bones of the dog
that must have starved to death either.
I never meant to find the innards of his life,
but there they were in the linen closet
under piles of clean sheets and towels.
These things weren't meant to be left behind
for some bitch like me to find.
I had no way to identify the destruction.
Now, I gasp for air
and trace my fingers over anonymous gravestones,
so I don't forget all the crack-pipe burns
on the tips of my fingers.

An Alcoholic Reflection

When I look at the mountain outside the library tower's window
I wonder which road leads to the top
and if anyone has traveled there without getting lost
or lonely. This moment reminds me of the taste of whiskey
and what I love about the past. All the glass bottles
I've emptied and tossed to the side of the road have changed
the landscape that I now claim as I sit in silence
behind stacks of books. Whatever else is happening in the world
suddenly matters and the sound of breaking glass turns me on.

The Smell Of Cigars

The silence between me and that cold glass of beer
on the kitchen table has been interrupted
by the men digging up the street
with jackhammers.

And the doorbell,
someone has been ringing my doorbell
for the last ten years.
Every time I go to answer it
no one is there.
Instead, there's a bag of Cheetos
half eaten
and the smell of cigars.

The men in the street keep digging.
The beer on the table created a disaster:
I have no pants on.
I'm standing in the middle of the street,
and the neighbor's dogs have been barking
at me since dawn.

There have been dogs running wild
since the dawn of time,
but now they're tied to lampposts
trying to get loose;
they are choking
and the men in the street
don't notice this either.

Looking For Lima Beans

When I stand in the frozen vegetable aisle
in the grocery store
looking for lima beans
I think of you suffering
trying to find one more drink
but you are in handcuffs now
and I don't have the key or magic to let you loose
I'm cursing and pacing back and forth
wondering where all the lima beans
are in this damn town
while you are trapped
in another town
where the birds growl and breathe heavy
where they serve you broken chickens
and starving cows for dinner
where the metal claws
cut off your circulation

I too want a bottle of whiskey
but I get frozen broccoli instead
they are out of lima beans

We both should have known
but we've mistaken family
for food and are starving
our bones are brittle

Behind Me Now

in line at the grocery store
is not just another person,
but an old man
waiting to pay for his prunes.
I notice the long wispy hairs
in his nose and ears and lose my appetite.

I didn't know all my neighbors
because no one mowed their lawns
or trimmed their bushes. They were afraid
to come outside.

When I was five
a man drove across the neighbor's lawn.
It was a reckless get away.

I saw his face in the rearview mirror,
his hairy nose was frightening;
it was like a monster crawling out of his head.
The black hairs like a thousand spider legs
took over his face.

Behind me now are monsters that look
like innocent old men standing in line.
I want to empty my grocery bag
and put it over their heads
to suffocate the memory
where all the houses appear empty,
all except an unmade bed,
or a refrigerator turned upside down

as if someone broke in and searched for an answer,
or a piece of jewelry or a child in a yellow sweater
waiting for her mother to come home.
This is what blooms in winter:
children sprout from yellowed linoleum floors
on Massachusetts Avenue.

In The News

Someone managed to take a picture
of that man pulled over on Felters Road.
He was missing a shoe and a few front teeth;
his face was covered in thick brown hair.
If pictures in the newspaper could smell
of anything other than cement,
this one would reek of piss and booze.

Yesterday, on my way home
I found myself pulled over
in front of the elementary school
on the corner of Conklin and Hayes
waiting for the kids to cross the street
and get on buses.
The crossing guard was reading the newspaper
when a gust of wind snatched the front page;
it spread across my windshield.
I couldn't see what was in front of me.
I couldn't tell if the car broke down or if it was me.
There were children screaming;
one of them stepped on my toe.
My hair was blowing in my eyes.

Some say the fire hydrants were sad that day;
others say this is what happens.

Sober Lunch Hours On 68th Street

A disappearing act without drinking
is like being trapped inside a chicken's egg,
the shell too hard to crack. The hours used me
and now I am living my life among the pigeons.
I wear white socks, cheap black or brown loafers,
try to get away with not wearing a bra.

I count chairs on floor plans at this dead end job;
the symbol for each chair a round black dot,
the center of a foggy pupil, an eye that's suffered
from starring down the barrel of a crack pipe
looking for rock but only finding resin,
not enough resin to catch fire,
to release the universe from paralysis.

These lunch hours are full of different versions of me
and sometimes everything in the world fits
into a three foot by three foot cubicle that stinks like an ashtray.
The salt in my tuna sandwiches and peeping pigeon sounds
last forever.

A Portrait

She walks down 83rd Street every morning
and talks to the flowers.
The flowers don't talk back to her
and in that silence
her circulation slows down, her fingers freeze.
She puts her hands in her pockets,
or maybe she looks over her shoulder
hoping to see her son picking himself up off the sidewalk,
peeling himself from the pavement like a candy wrapper
that's been tossed out a car window.
Nothing will break the silence;
hope will not free her son from prison.
The traffic light clicks and she crosses the street,
leaves her conversation with the flowers
and walks down to the Hudson.
She walks slowly into the river and listens
to the city, to the life she left behind.

This Is What People Do

What I notice now when I look at the world outside
is curtains. I mean I try to look outside, but the damn
curtains are always drawn shut. Most houses on the block
appear deserted.
In each house there's a bowl of water
in the corner of the living room,
an onion on the window's ledge,
and grandmothers on leashes
in front of a television.
This is what people do;
they die behind their own walls.
Every so often a grandmother gets loose.
She finds her way to the front door
beyond the beige curtains
and out into the street.
She finds the keys to the car and drives away.
Not knowing where to go,
she pulls into a gas station, fills the tank,
gets a pack of smokes,
and a hotdog for the road.
She drives around
until the loneliness
wears off.

The Sound Of Metal

is when the barrel of the shotgun slips through the blinds
after resting there all night.
When the street lamps flicker and turn off just before dawn,
the sound of metal is in the fist that's been holding tight,
and it is when the sky is half light and half dark
after the drugs are gone and the shaking hand
can no longer grip the gun nor hold the blinds apart
for long enough to see if the world has slipped away yet.
And the sound of metal scrapes against my chest.
The air solidifies as if to prevent the police
from entering and finding me
in the bathtub where I sleep and water drips
from the soles of my boots;
my feet are crying because I can't.
I wrap myself around the length of the shotgun.
I leave my fingerprints.

The Average Size Of Underwear Is Fifty-Two

In my home town, true love breeds in the neighbor's shrubs.
The average size of underwear is fifty-two.
Salesmen go door to door with empty briefcases.

The last time I drove through town,
there were more shoes on the side of the road than usual,
little girls' sneakers. It's like the children
are trying to outrun themselves and go missing.

The first time I left home I didn't go too far.
I didn't even wear shoes
when I ran down the stairs,
out the front door,
and past Mrs. Valenta.
I'll never forget
brushing up against
her fat butt and falling.
I remember spitting out dirt
and never wanting to go back
to Johnson City, New York,
where the little girls go missing,
where the bushes cry.

Driving Through Binghamton

On a Saturday morning,
I cross a bridge
and wonder about those men
down in the river,
waist deep in water.
I wonder if they are related to me.
Maybe one of my grandparents
had an affair.

I also wonder if the house
on Clinton Street,
the one that burned down
because a crack-head fell asleep on her pipe,
I wonder if anything was ever hidden in the walls
other than drugs or old newspapers.

When I drive through Binghamton,
I avoid Carroll Street
because in a previous life
I might have stood on the corner
and sold my body for an embarrassingly low price.

When I drive through town,
I look off into the distance
and recall the story about
when my grandfather was sold
to a farm so that his mother
had enough to eat.

Now, I see broken windows and old factories.
I see the places where my life was sewn together,
but I didn't know the clouds would shift,
and I would drive through the fog,
pulling myself apart at the seams,
looking for an old address
to see if anything other than my pants
were left behind.

In 2001 I Woke Up In The Dirt

A homeless man looks me dead in the eye,
whispers, *Al-Qaida Al-Qaida Al-Qiada.*
I'm pissed off he woke me up
in the middle of the afternoon.
When I lift my head from a pile of leaves,
a few stick to my cheek, stain it orange.
I must look like a pile of garbage.
I have no idea what this man is saying,
take a swig of warm beer
from the glass bottle under my shirt.
He tells me there's dirt in my drink;
it's cigarette butts and spit.
I must have found an empty bottle
of Old English 800 in someone's garbage
before making it to the park at dawn.
When I sleep outside, I always make sure
to have something glass to use as a weapon.

Under a tree just a couple of yards away
from the carousel and bandstand
that was replicated in Rod Serling's
Twilight Zone episode, "Walking Distance,"
I decide to surrender to my alcoholism,
convince myself that I am ready
to walk a certain distance.
By sundown, I forget that I make this decision,
wake up in the park the next day.
There are cigarette burns all over my hands
and I don't have anything to soothe the sting,
so I dig a little hole in the moist dirt with a stick,

bury my hands. I try to plant my limp fingers
in contaminated soil.

Louise Kutz

When you sat on the gold couch,
I never looked down at your fat ankles.
When you pulled every weed from your lawn,
I didn't pay attention.

I didn't pay attention to your hands,
nor did I look when you scooped vanilla ice cream
into a tall glass of 7up.

I never saw what you were made of,
not even when you were standing
on your driveway.

The red brick house waiting
for my arrival was eroding;
I couldn't see you aging.
The slabs of white cement
were too heavy and thick.
I was afraid you'd sink
as if it was quicksand.

On Wednesdays, when I'd visit,
even if you were too tired,
I never knew because this isn't what I looked for;
I only saw the gold couch and my reflection
in the plastic that covered it.

I never thought I'd want a gold sofa so badly,
and when I am alone,
usually at night,

I go outside and look around the backyard.
I look at the ground,
bend at the knees and get as close as I can
to see if you have been here before me.

Turnips

I empty my pockets when I get home,
and there they are—my dreams
sitting on the kitchen counter,
next to a bowl of water and dry cat food.

I don't question why there was cilantro
growing in the graveyard
where I spent the day,
wondering about your dreams.
How many of them were lost
or dug up or buried with you?

There's more than enough.
I think that's what you used to say,
but I never knew what that meant,
especially now when it feels like everything
is running out. I am guilty for my dripping faucet,
but the sound puts me to sleep. I am guilty
for the holes in my shoes and cold feet.

Guilt is what you fed me and now I am full.
In fact, I am sick to my stomach
and bored as I sit here running out of useless things
to pull out of my pockets. A couple of pennies
will get me nowhere closer to the dreams
you left in your top drawer next to your black socks.

If there is more than enough,
why have I confused my dreams
with my wishes? All the wishes

kept me drunk long enough, I didn't notice
I was standing in the garden speaking to the turnips.

Sunday Mornings

I never understood where the man's voice
came from on Sunday mornings
but it was just the neighbor cursing
his lawnmower for stalling again
I spoke to the dead bugs
trapped in the light fixture
and turned the table upside down
looking for evidence
It was like a robbery
when the burglar searches
every room and leaves everything behind
This is the way I lose sleep
I search for what's come before me
and clean up after myself
My mother is the only one I know
who mopped the floor
with a damp paper towel
She'd step on it and swipe
back and forth and leave streaks
She smeared her name on the floor
and turned everything to mud

Wonder Woman's Boobs

Wonder Woman's boobs meant a lot to me when I was growing up.
I mean, I wanted boobs like hers. So, I tried to grow a pair.
I drank a lot of milk, ate tons of chicken, and dreamt about
Wonder Woman and her boobs; I fell asleep holding my chest.
Sometimes I wore a tight t-shirt with Wonder Woman on it
and tried to fly chest first. I jumped off the roof of the garage
and broke my ankle.

It Takes A Lot Of Beer To Survive

I mean there's this guy,
Charlie,
who drinks a lot of beer
and rides in his wheelchair
up and down Main Street
all night.

Some people live too long
or their feet are wrapped
in strands of Christmas lights
that no longer light up.

But, Charlie's feet
rest on metal slats
as he pushes himself
through traffic.
He waits at every stop sign.

I am waiting for the day
we run out of gasoline
and have to push our memories
with our fat bodies.

Blue Balls

There's an old man inside of me who wants to scratch his balls.
I feel this itch every morning when I roll over in bed
and tell my wife that I love her.

There's not just one old man in me, but an army
of old bastards that try to get me to do things.

Like the time when I was twelve and stole my parents'
Volvo station wagon and robbed the mini-mart
on Ackley Ave. I tried to outrun the police;
they found my empty bottles of beer in the backseat.

One of the cops turned to the other and said,
This kid smells like an old man who smokes
too many cigarettes and drinks too much scotch.

The old men inside of me sit around
and play poker for pennies
like I used to with my grandmother.

They quit drinking, but every once in a while
I get a whiff of booze on someone's breath
and my old saggy men seem to like it.
I look inward and smile at them. I peek at their card hands.

I take a shower every night before I get in bed
and imagine the old men with blue balls.

Television Series

I've always wanted to be a part of *The Dick Van Dyke Show*
if I were Dick I'd come home from work early every day
lock the kid in the bedroom and make out with my wife
I mean I am sort of like Dick I'm a dyke
and my wife wears high heels and aprons around the house
our living room doesn't have carpet like Dick's house
we have hardwood floors and an old drunk lady
with a mullet lives downstairs

I've also wanted to be in *Three's Company*
to kick Jack out of the house

Poem In The Sand

C.K. Williams' poetry is so hot. I had a revelation in my pants; thank god it was silent and odorless because I was surrounded by poets. His poem about the girl who is wood and steel, holy shit, I've met the girl who is sticks and stones. And after he read the one titled, "This Happened," I almost fell out of my chair. After the reading I ran, I really walked, but my heart ran, out of the building. Twelfth Street smelled like filet mignon. I cried on the train ride home, but not because C.K. Williams' poetry turned me on. It did turn me on, but this is not why I cried. My senses were heightened; I am five feet four inches tall. His voice sounded like the first time I fell in love. Maybe it wasn't his voice, but the soft and hard sounds in his poems. My first broken heart too. I learned how to be less human, how to cry without crying, and to taste tears without tearing. I didn't make out with a farm animal or anything like that to learn this less than human feeling. It happened in Florida. A bald man introduced me and cocaine to each other. I haven't cried since my first love died, cocaine drowned and I made a grave in the sand on a beach in Sarasota. I taste tears every so often and try to remember what I wrote in the sand. Maybe it was just the date and time of her death.

I've Always Wanted To Be The Kind Of Boy

who could live up to the name Rocco
I'd wear white t-shirts and black jeans
work in a factory or drive a truck
and deliver soda to nursing homes
only to get familiar
with Mrs. Kutz and Mr. Fiaco
the lonely pair who sit on benches
and romanticize about the youth
that fills my pockets
as I strut by rolling a dolly
stacked high with cases of 7up
every Wednesday I'd tip the brim
of my newspaper boy hat
and say good morning
hoping they'd sit closer to each other
before the days slipped away
but they sat there without saying a word
until it was time for dinner
then they'd go inside
change their clothes
sip their sodas
complain about the pains
in their hands and fat knuckles
and they couldn't remember the names
of the days
somewhere a boy named Rocco
might be working with his hands
perhaps picking potatoes

or placing them on a conveyer belt
in a factory
wishing for a way out

White Cotton Underpants

I don't know her by name,
but I call her Janice.
She lived on the second floor
of the brownstone behind mine on 87th Street.
Every day she'd lie on the couch
I kept an eye on her,
worried about her when she'd get up
and go in the other room for too long.

I've always wanted to yell out
the name Janice in my bedroom,
but I'm afraid you'll take offense.

I think the lady that showed up late
to her book club at the bookstore,
I think her name was Janice.
I think all the women were named Janice,
they kept saying, *hi Janice,*
hi Janice.

Janice wrote an article in the newspaper
about another woman named Janice,
this Janice quit her job as City Clerk in Burke County
when New York State passed the Marriage Equality Act.
I wonder where Janice lives now
or if she'll wear a t-shirt and white cotton underpants
and lie on the couch all day.

The Fish With Feet

I waited for the fish to grow feet
because I thought this would prove
what it means to be human,
but the damn thing kept circling its bowl.

This, I thought, this must be how mothers love,
and I wanted to learn this love
so I'd spend nights staring at the damn fish.
Every so often it would make bubbles.
I would grip the bowl, press my face against the glass,
and look as hard as I could at its yellow-orange belly
to see if its feet were finally going to sprout.

The porch light shining through my bedroom window
cast a halo-shaped shadow over the fishbowl
as if to protect my experiment with love.

When the patio light no longer turned on or off,
I grew tired of waiting and tried to grow gills.

Ode To Leroy Street

Leroy drives the bus that stops
on the corner where the woman wearing hot
pink sweatpants drops quarters on the sidewalk;
her name is Leroy, too.

Another guy named Leroy
stands outside of the liquor store
at 7:55 am.

I think my name should be Leroy
because every time I look out my window
buses pass by and yellow electric letters
flash "Leroy Street," "Leroy Street."
At the stop light
next to the liquor store
next to hot-pink-sweatpants-Leroy
bending at the knees

there are kids sitting with their backs
facing the street.
I can't hear what they are saying
from over here on the second floor;
I imagine them whispering
No, Leroy. Leroy, no,
don't leave.

Kids On The Southside

There are little boys with nicknames
like Old-Man Joe and Gramps
hanging onto the chain-linked fence.
It's like they are on the inside of the belly,
trapped in their own guts looking out.
Their arms and legs scorched from lit cigarettes
and car lighters.

I don't know how boys survive
when their hands are nailed to the walls
of Johnson City, New York, where people like me
are considered road kill for these kids to play with.

When they crawl through the hole in the fence
they are born again and I can hardly breathe.

Uncle Mike Used To Watch Flies Explode

Uncle Mike worked the night shift in the 70's;
without gloves, he dipped motherboards or some sort of circuits
into purple chemicals. He usually laughs a little
when he gets to the part about how he's surprised he didn't explode.
The chemicals seeped into the flies, into the land, into the men,
and into the tomatoes and gardens that line the hills
up the street from IBM's factory, but only the flies burst.
Everything is still rotting on the stem.
Our holiday dinners were not what stained the counter tops
and oven. The red splatter was not mom's homemade sauce;
it was blood from the gardens, little drops of tomato blood,
crusted over and burnt into the unprotected skin of our lives.

Traffic

The traffic on 88th Street and Broadway
has me wanting to stick a needle in my arm.
That's all it will take—they tell me—the lack
of willingness to sit at a red light.

There are men that smell like a barroom,
who keep showing up under my pillow.
In the middle of the night they pat my forehead
with a cool damp cloth, tell me how the traffic
isn't so bad at the bottom of the Hudson River.

On 88th Street the buildings melt like lava
and an old woman carries a brown paper bag,
filled to the brim, doesn't notice the ring of heat.
When she turns the corner I disappear with her.
On days like this I pretend
that the scars have completely healed.

The View From The Top Of The Ferris Wheel At The Johnson City Field Days

There were a dozen kids in the bathroom,
waiting for the tub to fill with water.
I saw them when I walked into the third floor apartment
to buy drugs. Their father, with long blond hair in his eyes,
walked passed me, pissed in the bathwater.

I should have robbed that family,
kidnapped the little boy who grabbed my leg,
squeezed like I was his mother.
Every drug deal was this desperate
on the street behind the old Price Chopper,
where all the houses are on fire
and food stamps float in the air with the ashes.
This is where I used to go to rip myself off,
where blue-eyed children ride bicycles
through flames that have been lighting up the sky
for the last twenty years.

I've Got The World On A String

I ran through the living room in dad's loafers and black suit,
belting Frank Sinatra's "I've Got The World On A String"
into a broomstick, and when I look at your feet,
sticking out of your orange jumpsuit, I remember what it was like
to put on dad's grey socks and tighten my suspenders. I wish I could
give you this costume; it made me feel like a tough guy.

Now, in the visiting room at the Brooklyn Detention Center,
you sit next to dad, describe the pains in your feet. You say
how there are no toenails left and when you were arrested
you weren't wearing any shoes. One foot the size of an elephant,
ten-thousand dollars duct taped to your leg. And I can only imagine
how ugly the visiting room is and how there's probably a stain on the ceiling
that looks like a chicken with its head cut off.

The Cemetery On Riverside Drive

The cemetery on Riverside Drive is emptying out;
they are just getting up from their graves to go to work,
or war, or to get some Chinese food across the street.
I'm standing in line behind a dead guy,
waiting for sesame chicken and wonton soup.
We both smell like dirt, our faces and knees grass stained.
The air smells like vinegar and river water. I've swallowed
too much violence, mud is stuck in my throat.

I never should have carved my name into the fencepost
that marked the property line, divided the differences
between the death that my brother continues to eat
alone in the prison yard and the hope that we pumped
into our veins when we used to break into graveyards
in the middle of the night for no reason other than to guard
the cracked headstones, catch fireflies, suffocate them in jars.
We've earned these little flashes of light together.

Driving Yourself To Jail In July

This morning you called to tell me that you were driving yourself to jail
for breaking probation, that drug court warned you about poppy seed bagels,
and the news reported about how the roads are in desperate need of repair
in Johnson City, how there is no money in the budget to fix them.
The news reporter stood over a pothole the size of a grave,
the camera zoomed in on the broken pavement. A man
in a wheelchair waited to cross the street in the background.
I told you to call me when you get out next Tuesday,
that we can meet to talk about what we'll need to visit the dead,
that it might be a good idea to remember the smell of jail—
not to confuse your Newport cigarettes for freedom
and that the cold floor in the shower might be a good place to stand
if you feel lonely. And, you said there was a bottle of whiskey
in the trunk of your car that might explode if it gets too hot this week.

The Gypsies Were Always In Town

According to my mother,
these gypsies were like mosquitos
or wasps—insects that hunt.

She said that I'd better watch out,
so I hung flypaper from the ceiling
to see if gypsies would stick.

I'd sit alone at dusk
and try to catch the gypsies
and my mother's threats.

There was this one gypsy
that lit up in a jar beside my bed;
his name was Charlie.
One night he broke out of the jar,
tied my feet to the bedpost.
Charlie must have had too much to drink.

Sometimes I get a whiff of booze
and it reminds me of the night I met Charlie,
the night I trapped the moon in a jar.

Children's Books

The farmer who falls asleep with a cigarette in his hand
is not in the picture with the skinny blue cow.

It's not that bad having a blue face, or being the cow that starves,
because spring is almost here and everyone is about to get fat.

I've been sitting next to a kid at the library for an hour,
flipping through books with illustrations that don't make sense.

Not only are the cows blue and starving, but the dogs are red
and the grass is bright yellow.

At the end of the book, the bushes are green
and I am jealous of how fast they come to life.

I feel like I am trapped in the book about farmers and birds,
trapped inside the little birdhouse that some punk set on fire.

I want to tell this kid that the doors don't have knobs,
that the smoke is about to thicken.

My finger nails are too short to pry us out.

America, Let's Pretend Your Name Is George

Dear George,
There are lesbians wearing their grandmother's wedding dresses.
George, why do I want to kiss your belly? This desire feels
incestuous. George, I'm listening to Christmas music in July and
frying your chicken. I'm hungry, standing in the banana aisle at the
grocery store, pretending to pick up the lemons that fell so I can
get a better look at my teacher's legs; she shops here too. George,
of course I am going to be a poet. I drank all your beer before I
turned nine. George, your kids smell like mustard and hotdogs.
Please keep them on a leash. George, there is no more room for
any more elephants. George, when I find out I am pregnant, we'll
celebrate, and we'll find a cure for your allergies. George, I went to
the doctor and he said the glaciers are melting in Juneau, Alaska,
and I'm worried we may be stuck here forever, where people are
dying. George, I will cover you in plastic and get Walt Whitman
to let us on his ferry. George, get out of bed, all of this is
happening and I just want to be left alone. George, your leather
belt is too tight and your ass looks sexy in those pants. George, I've
inherited my grandfather's shotguns, thanks to you.

Getting In The Backseat With Charles Bukowski

If I could have my way I'd sit on a barstool
and stare at the background through the bottoms
of beer bottles,
but this is something I don't let people know
especially all those people at the university
who eat too many cookies for breakfast
and show up to class early.
If things were different,
I'd be spinning around in circles
on a barstool,
excited,
so excited my vagina would smile,
and if I wore tight pants you'd see the grin.
I'm just sayin',
if I were to have my way one more time
it might get me drunk
and I'd imagine sitting in the backseat
of an Oldsmobile with Charles Bukowski,
wondering why the car is not moving
and what time the bar opens.

The Aluminum Grave

I wouldn't have known to look under the table,
if you hadn't left a note on the refrigerator door.
Even though it's unplugged and turned upside down,
your note, the one you wrote last year, and taped to the freezer door,
hasn't moved. I would never have remembered to turn off the stove,
water the plants, pay the phone bill, brush my teeth, or look
under the table to find all the empty beer cans;
the aluminum grave smells of urine.
I never would have found the box of ashes,
your cigarette ashes, the ones I emptied
in the garbage the day you died.

The Order Of Creation

my brother punched my father in the face
but not in the face with his fist
in his head with a baseball bat
on his back with a belt
in his shin with a cleat
on his arm with a stick

my brother whaled my mother
in the head with his knuckles   they broke
he punched so hard he passed out
and didn't wake up

I didn't wake up either
we planned to meet
under the bed
where the cat hid when it rained
where we found the dog dead

If You Are Addicted To Binghamton

the cuts on the bottom of your feet burn
when you walk through parking lots
when you bathe in the Susquehanna
when you go fishing in your neighbor's pool
the blowup pool that sits in the front yard
where blades of grass
and the meaning of an entire day
bake in the sun
If you are addicted to Binghamton
then you are probably related to someone
who belongs to the Knights of Columbus
someone who knows my grandfather
who knows a cop
who knows someone that ran a red light
on Main Street across from St. James
on their way home from the bar
that I was born in
If you are addicted to Binghamton
try drinking a glass of water
with your back against the front door
try not to starve your houseplants
try not to give up on your house
If you are addicted to Binghamton
you'll need some assistance from the government
try not to have more than seven children
running around the pool on your front lawn
If you are addicted to Binghamton
you're probably addicted to the sounds
smash bang boom

Johnson City

The neighbor's dog won't stop barking

and the bear at the zoo is pacing
back and forth

The old lady on the couch has not moved
since last February

I see her through my bedroom window

My wife tells me to shut up
at just the right moment

This is Johnson City

The deck needs to be washed
it is moldy from dog piss

The shoebox in the closet is empty

There are blank toe tags and broken chairs
for sale on front lawns in this town

This is Johnson City

Old ladies sweep their porches
then the sidewalks

The K Mart has bedbugs
the people don't know why they have syphilis

They wait for five o'clock in this town
they stand in traffic and wait for a miracle

Acknowledgments

Thanks to the journals and websites in which these poems, or a version of these poems, have appeared:

Hawaii Pacific Review: "Santalucia"
The Cincinnati Review: "The Crack House"
So to Speak: "Jealousy"
Poetrybay: "The Prisoner"
The Long Islander Newspaper: "A Portrait"
2 Bridges Review: "In Other Words"
Paterson Literary Review: "Looking For Lima Beans," "In Johnson City Not All Of The Houses Have Basements," "Turnips," "The Aluminum Grave," "Louise Kutz," "Traffic," and "The Coffee Table"
Gertrude Press: "Bitches On The Roof" and "The View From The Top Of The Ferris Wheel At The Johnson City Field Days"
Clockhouse Review: "I've Always Wanted To Be The Kind of Boy"
Ragazine cc: "The Things I Want To Believe," "Behind Me Now," and "Emptying Out The House"
Bayou Magazine: "Poem In The Sand"
The Inquisitive Eater: New School Food: "The Cannoli Machine At The Brooklyn Detention Center," "Dear America" re-titled "America, Let's Pretend Your Name Is George," and "Oh Brother"
Pax Americana: "Witness Of Consumption"
Oklahoma Review: "Kids On The Southside"

Many poems in this collection appeared in the chapbook *Driving Yourself to Jail in July* (Dead Bison Press, 2014).

ABOUT THE AUTHOR

NICOLE SANTALUCIA is a recipient of the Ruby Irene Poetry Chapbook Prize from *Arcadia Magazine* for her manuscript, *Driving Yourself to Jail in July* (2014) and the 2015 Edna St. Vincent Millay Poetry Prize from the *Tishman Review*. She received a Creative Writing Fellowship from the Marion Clayton Link Endowment, a Chancellor's Award and a Council Foundation Award for Service from Binghamton University.

Her non-fiction and poetry have appeared in publications such as *The Cincinnati Review, Paterson Literary Review, Hawaii Pacific Review, 2 Bridges Review, Bayou Magazine, Gertrude, Flyway: Journal of Writing and Environment, So to Speak: A Feminist Journal of Language and Art,* as well as numerous other journals. Santalucia received her M.F.A. from The New School University and her Ph.D. in English from Binghamton University. She founded The Binghamton Poetry Project, a literary outreach program that reaches underserved audiences, and she directed the program for four years. She currently teaches at Shippensburg University in Pennsylvania and brings poetry workshops into the Cumberland County Prison.

VIA FOLIOS
A refereed book series dedicated to the culture of Italians and Italian Americans.

MARK CIABATTARI. *Preludes to History.* Vol 114 Poetry. $12

HELEN BAROLINI. *Visits.* Vol 113 Novel. $22

ERNESTO LIVORNI. *The Fathers' America.* Vol 112 Poetry. $16

MARIO B. MIGNONE. *The Story of My People.* Vol 111 Non-fiction. $17

GEORGE GUIDA. *The Sleeping Gulf.* Vol 110 Poetry. $14

JOEY NICOLETTI. *Reverse Graffiti.* Vol 109 Poetry. $14

GIOSE RIMANELLI. *Il mestiere del furbo.* Vol 108 Criticism. $20

LEWIS TURCO. *The Hero Enkido.* Vol 107 Poetry. $14

AL TACCONELLI. *Perhaps Fly.* Vol 106 Poetry. $14

RACHEL GUIDO DEVRIES. *A Woman Unknown in her Bones.* Vol 105 Poetry. $11

BERNARD BRUNO. *A Tear and a Tear in My Heart.* Vol 104 Non-fiction. $20

FELIX STEFANILE. *Songs of the Sparrow.* Vol 103 Poetry. $30

FRANK POLIZZI. *A New Life with Bianca.* Vol 102 Poetry. $10

GIL FAGIANI. *Stone Walls.* Vol 101 Poetry. $14

LOUISE DESALVO. *Casting Off.* Vol 100 Fiction. $22

MARY JO BONA. *I stop waiting for You.* Vol 99 Poetry. $12

RACHEL GUIDO DEVRIES. *Stati zitt, Josie.* Vol 98 Children's Literature. $8

GRACE CAVALIERI. *The Mandate of Heaven.* Vol 97 Poetry. $14

MARISA FRASCA. *Via incanto.* Vol 96 Poetry. $12

DOUGLAS GLADSTONE. *Carving a Niche for Himself.* Vol 95 History. $12

MARIA TERRONE. *Eye to Eye.* Vol 94 Poetry. $14

CONSTANCE SANCETTA. *Here in Cerchio* Vol 93 Local History. $15

MARIA MAZZIOTTI GILLAN. *Ancestors' Song* Vol 92 Poetry. $14

DARRELL FUSARO. *What if Godzilla Just Wanted a Hug?* Vol ? Essays. $TBA

MICHAEL PARENTI. *Waiting for Yesterday: Pages from a Street Kid's Life.* Vol 90 Memoir. $15

ANNIE LANZILOTTO, *Schistsong*, Vol. 89. Poetry, $15

EMANUEL DI PASQUALE, *Love Lines*, Vol. 88. Poetry, $10

CAROSONE & LOGIUDICE. *Our Naked Lives.* Vol 87 Essays. $15

JAMES PERICONI. *Strangers in a Strange Land: A Survey of Italian-Language American Books.* Vol. 86. Book History. $24

DANIELA GIOSEFFI, *Escaping La Vita Della Cucina*, Vol. 85. Essays & Creative Writing. $22

MARIA FAMÀ, *Mystics in the Family*, Vol. 84. Poetry, $10

ROSSANA DEL ZIO, *From Bread and Tomatoes to Zuppa di Pesce "Ciambotto"*, Vol. 83. $15

LORENZO DELBOCA, *Polentoni*, Vol. 82. Italian Studies, $15

SAMUEL GHELLI, *A Reference Grammar*, Vol. 81. Italian Language. $36

ROSS TALARICO, *Sled Run*, Vol. 80. Fiction. $15

FRED MISURELLA, *Only Sons*, Vol. 79. Fiction. $14

FRANK LENTRICCHIA, *The Portable Lentricchia*, Vol. 78. Fiction. $16

RICHARD VETERE, *The Other Colors in a Snow Storm*, Vol. 77. Poetry. $10

GARIBALDI LAPOLLA, *Fire in the Flesh*, Vol. 76 Fiction & Criticism. $25

GEORGE GUIDA, *The Pope Stories*, Vol. 75 Prose. $15

ROBERT VISCUSI, *Ellis Island*, Vol. 74. Poetry. $28

ELENA GIANINI BELOTTI, *The Bitter Taste of Strangers Bread*, Vol. 73, Fiction, $24

PINO APRILE, *Terroni*, Vol. 72, Italian Studies, $20

Bordighera Press is an imprint of Bordighera, Incorporated, an independently owned not-for-profit scholarly organization that has no legal affiliation with the University of Central Florida or with The John D. Calandra Italian American Institute, Queens College/CUNY.

EMANUEL DI PASQUALE, *Harvest*, Vol. 71, Poetry, $10

ROBERT ZWEIG, *Return to Naples*, Vol. 70, Memoir, $16

AIROS & CAPPELLI, *Guido*, Vol. 69, Italian/American Studies, $12

FRED GARDAPHÉ, *Moustache Pete is Dead! Long Live Moustache Pete!*, Vol. 67, Literature/Oral History, $12

PAOLO RUFFILLI, *Dark Room/Camera oscura*, Vol. 66, Poetry, $11

HELEN BAROLINI, *Crossing the Alps*, Vol. 65, Fiction, $14

COSMO FERRARA, *Profiles of Italian Americans*, Vol. 64, Italian Americana, $16

GIL FAGIANI, *Chianti in Connecticut*, Vol. 63, Poetry, $10

BASSETTI & D'ACQUINO, *Italic Lessons*, Vol. 62, Italian/American Studies, $10

CAVALIERI & PASCARELLI, Eds., *The Poet's Cookbook*, Vol. 61, Poetry/Recipes, $12

EMANUEL DI PASQUALE, *Siciliana*, Vol. 60, Poetry, $8

NATALIA COSTA, Ed., *Bufalini*, Vol. 59, Poetry. $18.

RICHARD VETERE, *Baroque*, Vol. 58, Fiction. $18.

LEWIS TURCO, *La Famiglia/The Family*, Vol. 57, Memoir, $15

NICK JAMES MILETI, *The Unscrupulous*, Vol. 56, Humanities, $20

BASSETTI, ACCOLLA, D'AQUINO, *Italici: An Encounter with Piero Bassetti*, Vol. 55, Italian Studies, $8

GIOSE RIMANELLI, *The Three-legged One*, Vol. 54, Fiction, $15

CHARLES KLOPP, *Bele Antiche Stòrie*, Vol. 53, Criticism, $25

JOSEPH RICAPITO, *Second Wave*, Vol. 52, Poetry, $12

GARY MORMINO, *Italians in Florida*, Vol. 51, History, $15

GIANFRANCO ANGELUCCI, *Federico F.*, Vol. 50, Fiction, $15

ANTHONY VALERIO, *The Little Sailor*, Vol. 49, Memoir, $9

ROSS TALARICO, *The Reptilian Interludes*, Vol. 48, Poetry, $15

RACHEL GUIDO DE VRIES, *Teeny Tiny Tino's Fishing Story*, Vol. 47, Children's Literature, $6

EMANUEL DI PASQUALE, *Writing Anew*, Vol. 46, Poetry, $15

MARIA FAMÀ, *Looking For Cover*, Vol. 45, Poetry, $12

ANTHONY VALERIO, *Toni Cade Bambara's One Sicilian Night*, Vol. 44, Poetry, $10

EMANUEL CARNEVALI, Dennis Barone, Ed., *Furnished Rooms*, Vol. 43, Poetry, $14

BRENT ADKINS, et al., Ed., *Shifting Borders, Negotiating Places*, Vol. 42, Proceedings, $18

GEORGE GUIDA, *Low Italian*, Vol. 41, Poetry, $11

GARDAPHÈ, GIORDANO, TAMBURRI, *Introducing Italian Americana*, Vol. 40, Italian/American Studies, $10

DANIELA GIOSEFFI, *Blood Autumn/Autunno di sangue*, Vol. 39, Poetry, $15/$25

FRED MISURELLA, *Lies to Live by*, Vol. 38, Stories, $15

STEVEN BELLUSCIO, *Constructing a Bibliography*, Vol. 37, Italian Americana, $15

ANTHONY JULIAN TAMBURRI, Ed., *Italian Cultural Studies 2002*, Vol. 36, Essays, $18

BEA TUSIANI, *con amore*, Vol. 35, Memoir, $19

FLAVIA BRIZIO-SKOV, Ed., *Reconstructing Societies in the Aftermath of War*, Vol. 34, History, $30

TAMBURRI, et al., Eds., *Italian Cultural Studies 2001*, Vol. 33, Essays, $18

ELIZABETH G. MESSINA, Ed., *In Our Own Voices*, Vol. 32, Italian/American Studies, $25

STANISLAO G. PUGLIESE, *Desperate Inscriptions*, Vol. 31, History, $12

HOSTERT & TAMBURRI, Eds., *Screening Ethnicity*, Vol. 30, Italian/American Culture, $25

G. PARATI & B. LAWTON, Eds., *Italian Cultural Studies*, Vol. 29, Essays, $18

HELEN BAROLINI, *More Italian Hours*, Vol. 28, Fiction, $16

FRANCO NASI, Ed., *Intorno alla Via Emilia*, Vol. 27, Culture, $16

ARTHUR L. CLEMENTS, *The Book of Madness & Love*, Vol. 26, Poetry, $10

JOHN CASEY, et al., *Imagining Humanity*, Vol. 25, Interdisciplinary Studies, $18

ROBERT LIMA, *Sardinia/Sardegna*, Vol. 24, Poetry, $10

DANIELA GIOSEFFI, *Going On*, Vol. 23, Poetry, $10

ROSS TALARICO, *The Journey Home*, Vol. 22, Poetry, $12

EMANUEL DI PASQUALE, *The Silver Lake Love Poems*, Vol. 21, Poetry, $7

JOSEPH TUSIANI, *Ethnicity*, Vol. 20, Poetry, $12

JENNIFER LAGIER, *Second Class Citizen*, Vol. 19, Poetry, $8

FELIX STEFANILE, *The Country of Absence*, Vol. 18, Poetry, $9

PHILIP CANNISTRARO, *Blackshirts*, Vol. 17, History, $12

LUIGI RUSTICHELLI, Ed., *Seminario sul racconto*, Vol. 16, Narrative, $10

LEWIS TURCO, *Shaking the Family Tree*, Vol. 15, Memoirs, $9

LUIGI RUSTICHELLI, Ed., *Seminario sulla drammaturgia*, Vol. 14, Theater/Essays, $10

FRED GARDAPHÈ, *Moustache Pete is Dead! Long Live Moustache Pete!*, Vol. 13, Oral Literature, $10

JONE GAILLARD CORSI, *Il libretto d'autore*, 1860–1930, Vol. 12, Criticism, $17

HELEN BAROLINI, *Chiaroscuro: Essays of Identity*, Vol. 11, Essays, $15

PICARAZZI & FEINSTEIN, Eds., *An African Harlequin in Milan*, Vol. 10, Theater/Essays, $15

JOSEPH RICAPITO, *Florentine Streets & Other Poems*, Vol. 9, Poetry, $9

FRED MISURELLA, *Short Time*, Vol. 8, Novella, $7

NED CONDINI, *Quartettsatz*, Vol. 7, Poetry, $7

ANTHONY JULIAN TAMBURRI, Ed., *Fuori: Essays by Italian/American Lesbians and Gays*, Vol. 6, Essays, $10

ANTONIO GRAMSCI, P. Verdicchio, Trans. & Intro. , *The Southern Question*, Vol. 5, Social Criticism, $5

DANIELA GIOSEFFI, *Word Wounds & Water Flowers*, Vol. 4, Poetry, $8

WILEY FEINSTEIN, *Humility's Deceit: Calvino Reading Ariosto Reading Calvino*, Vol. 3, Criticism, $10

PAOLO A. GIORDANO, Ed., *Joseph Tusiani: Poet, Translator, Humanist*, Vol. 2, Criticism, $25

ROBERT VISCUSI, *Oration Upon the Most Recent Death of Christopher Columbus*, Vol. 1, Poetry, $3

www.ingramcontent.com/pod-product-compliance
Lightning Source LLC
LaVergne TN
LVHW041302080426
835510LV00009B/836